BLAZERS

The World's Deadliest

The Deadliest Places on Earth

by Connie Colwell Miller

Reading Consultant:
Barbara J. Fox
Reading Specialist
North Carolina State University

Content Consultant:
Harold A. Perkins, PhD
Assistant Professor
Department of Geography
Ohio University, Athens

Blazers is published by Capstone Press,
151 Good Counsel Drive, P.O. Box 669, Mankato, Minnesota 56002.
www.capstonepress.com

092009
005619WZS10

Books published by Capstone Press are manufactured with paper
containing at least 10 percent post-consumer waste.

Library of Congress Cataloging-in-Publication Data
Miller, Connie Colwell, 1976–
  The deadliest places on earth / by Connie Colwell Miller.
    p. cm. — (Blazers. The world's deadliest.)
  Includes bibliographical references and index.
  Summary: "Describes deadly places and what makes them dangerous"— Provided
by publisher.
  ISBN 978-1-4296-3932-3 (library binding)
  1. Natural disasters — Juvenile literature. 2. Hazardous geographic environments — Juvenile
literature. I. Title. II. Series.
GB5019.M55 2010
904'.5 — dc22   2009032779

Editorial Credits

Kathryn Clay, editor; Matt Bruning, designer; Svetlana Zhurkin, media researcher;
  Laura Manthe, production specialist

Photo Credits

TABLE OF CONTENTS

DEADLY PLACES

Danger can be found all over the planet. Under the ocean. On top of a mountain. In the middle of a desert. The deadliest place of all might surprise you.

SORT OF DANGEROUS

DANGER
Meter

DISAPPEARING ACT

The Bermuda Triangle is a strange area in the Atlantic Ocean. Hundreds of ships and planes have disappeared here. No one knows what happens to them or to the people inside them.

DEADLY FACT

Disappearances in the Bermuda Triangle have been blamed on poor weather and pilot error.

UNDER THE SEA

Thousands of sea creatures live in the ocean. But oceans can be deadly places for people. Huge waves can pull people overboard. Rough ocean waters can sink ships.

DEADLY **FACT**

Shark attacks are rare but can be deadly.

RING OF FIRE

Red-hot **magma** surrounds the Pacific Ocean. This area is called the Pacific Ring of Fire. It is more than 25,000 miles (40,000 kilometers) long. Most of the world's deadly volcanoes are found here.

DEADLY FACT

More than 400 volcanoes are in the Pacific Ring of Fire.

magma – melted rock found under the earth's surface

DEADLY SWAMP

Snapping crocodiles and alligators **lurk** in the swampy Florida Everglades. Deadly pythons slither through the **marsh**. One wrong step here and you could become dinner.

lurk – to lie hidden

marsh – an area of wet, low land where grasses grow

Chapter 3

VERY DANGEROUS

DEADLY DOWNPOURS

Mother Nature is no friend to Taiwan. The Asian island experiences more than 200 earthquakes each year. Quakes cause buildings to tumble.

DEADLY FACT

Heavy rainfall creates deadly floods and landslides in Taiwan.

WATER PLEASE

The Sahara is the largest hot desert in the world. The sand is scorching. People who try to cross the desert may die of **dehydration**.

DEADLY *FACT*

The Sahara holds the hottest temperature on record. In 1922, this desert reached 136 degrees Fahrenheit (57.8 degrees Celsius).

dehydration – a health condition caused by lack of water

DIRTY AND DEADLY

If you think your room is dirty, then you haven't seen the city of Baku, Azerbaijan (ah-zer-bahy-JAHN). Baku is one of the dirtiest places on earth. The air is filled with smog. Oil spills pollute the water.

DEADLY *FACT*

Baku's water supply is also polluted by chemicals used to grow cotton.

19

DEADLY JUNGLE

The Amazon rain forest is home to deadly mosquitoes and flies. These insects spread **malaria**. Malaria can cause fever, chills, and death.

DEADLY *FACT*

Malaria kills more than 1 million people each year.

malaria - a serious disease that people get from mosquito bites

Chapter 4

EXTREMELY DANGEROUS

ANIMAL ATTACKS

The Great Barrier Reef near Australia is home to beautiful sea life. But some sea animals are deadly. Jellyfish and the blue-ringed octopus have **venom**. The venom can kill a person in minutes.

venom - poisonous liquid produced by some animals

FREEZING TO DEATH

Antarctica is the coldest and windiest place on earth. Freezing temperatures of -100 degrees Fahrenheit (-73 degrees Celsius) keep most people away. Visitors risk **frostbite**.

DEADLY FACT

Antarctica's cold temperatures can kill a person in less than one hour.

frostbite - a condition that occurs when cold temperatures freeze skin

TOP THAT

Annapurna in the Himalayas is a dangerous mountain. People climb this mountain for sport. But extreme weather and falls from rocky cliffs kill many climbers.

DEADLY *FACT*

Many people have tried to climb Annapurna. Nearly 40 percent have died while trying.

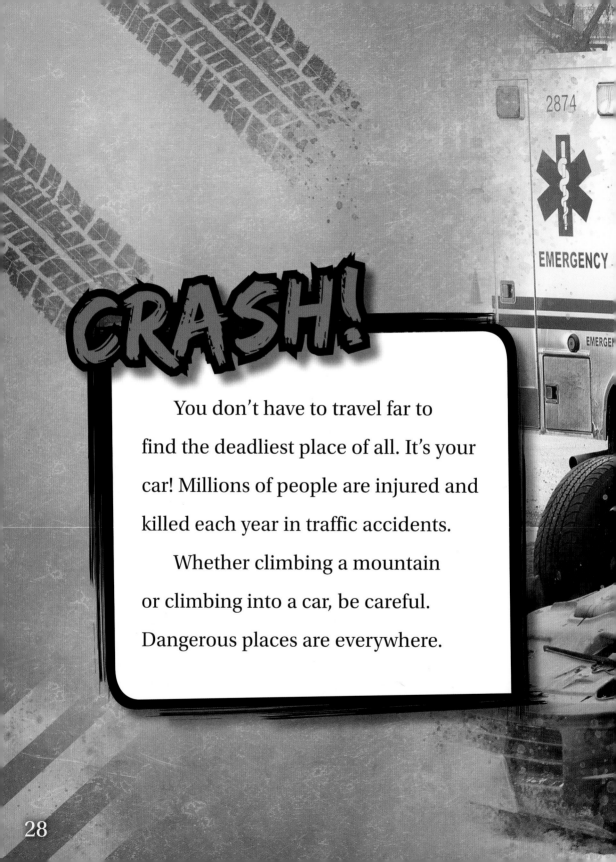

CRASH!

You don't have to travel far to find the deadliest place of all. It's your car! Millions of people are injured and killed each year in traffic accidents.

Whether climbing a mountain or climbing into a car, be careful. Dangerous places are everywhere.

GLOSSARY

dehydration (dee-hy-DRAY-shuhn) — a health condition caused by lack of water

frostbite (FRAWST-byt) — a condition that occurs when cold temperatures freeze skin

landslide (LAND-slide) — a large mass of earth and rocks that suddenly slides down a mountain or hill

lurk (LURK) — to lie hidden

magma (MAG-muh) — melted rock found under the earth's surface

malaria (muh-LAIR-ee-ah) — a disease that people get from mosquito bites; malaria causes high fever, chills, and sometimes death.

marsh (MARSH) — an area of wet, low land where grasses grow

venom (VEN-uhm) — poisonous liquid produced by some animals

READ MORE

Mason, Paul. *The World's Most Dangerous Places.* Atomic. Chicago: Raintree, 2007.

Sandler, Michael. *Mountains: Surviving on Mt. Everest.* X-Treme Places. New York: Bearport, 2006.

Walker, Kathryn. *Mysteries of the Bermuda Triangle.* Unsolved! New York: Crabtree, 2009.

INTERNET SITES

FactHound offers a safe, fun way to find Internet sites related to this book. All of the sites on FactHound have been researched by our staff.

Here's all you do:

Visit *www.facthound.com*

FactHound will fetch the best sites for you!

INDEX